BONES AND ASH

Ma Jaya Sati Bhagavati

BONES AND ASH

Ma Jaya Sati Bhagavati

1995

JAYA PRESS
Sebastian, Florida

JAYA PRESS
11155 Roseland Rd. #10
Sebastian, FL 32958

Editor: Brahma Das / Richard Rosenkranz
Layout & Design: Nirmal
Illustrations: Ma Jaya Sati Bhagavati
Cover Art: *Shiva*, by Ma, 1990

Copyright © 1995 by the Kashi Foundation

Publisher's Cataloging in Publication
(Prepared by Quality Books Inc.)
Ma, Jaya Sati Bhagavati.
Bones and ash / Jaya Sati Bhagavati Ma.
p. cm.
ISBN 0-9640469-2-X
ISBN 0-9640469-3-8 (pbk.)

I. Title.
PS3563.M353B66 1995   811'.54
                              QBI94-21205

First Printing: December 1995

Appreciation to Zelda Rosenkranz for her generous assistance.

To my Billy

His is the spirit
that walks in the Mother's shadow
unafraid to love
He is the spirit
that loves to love
Memories of the past
fill my soul
I am his Ma

Book 43

TABLE OF CONTENTS

INTRODUCTION

Between November, 1991, and October, 1992, Ma Jaya Sati Bhagavati wrote eighty-nine journals entitled *Bones and Ash* as a memorial, a tribute to Dr. Thomas "Billy" Byrom.

Billy was an Oxford Don and taught at Harvard. He was a gifted author and he co-founded, with Ma, the River School. Ma's first student, Billy was a man of enormous heart and compassion.

Ma spoke to Billy in these journals, continuing conversations with him on God and love and death and life. She pasted photos on every other page and spoke from her grief at his passing and her joy at his presence.

As with everything Ma does or writes or paints, she shared these private books with her students. Reading them was one of the most profound experiences of my life, and I was unable to read more than a few pages at a time. I was swimming in a sea of universal truths, and the deeper I swam, the deeper and more beautiful the truths. After many requests, Ma agreed to share the journals with the general public.

Working on *Bones and Ash* has been a labor of love for me. Ma has been my guru for over twenty years, and Billy was my friend and mentor.

Even though Ma wasn't writing poetry, all the *Bones and Ash* books were poetry to me. With her permission, I formed the prose into stanzas and grouped them into chapters.

The illustrations in this book are taken from Ma's early work as an artist. The cover painting of Shiva was done in 1989 and was one of Billy's favorites.

As many times as I've read these poems, even now I get intoxicated on their beauty and can only read a few at a time. I'm grateful to Ma and to Billy for this treasure.

Brahma Das
Kashi Ashram
December, 1995

Bones and Ash

The Ash

I wear the ash when my heart is broken
I wear the ash when my heart is full
I wear the ash for all the dead
I wear the ash for those alive
I wear the ash just for me

The Bones

The secret of the cremation grounds
is in the bones
before the fire turns them to ash

The bones feed the fire their life's moments
and surrender their ash to the Wind God

Please don't clutter my cremation grounds
with negative thoughts

Keep the burning pyre always burning
leaving only ash behind
not ego thoughts of negativity

The Way to Curb Judgment

The way to curb judgment
whether subtle or gross
is always to ask
Would I want to be judged as I judge?

Every life is unique
What possesses one person to act one way
is very different
for the next person
That is the beauty of death
in the cremation grounds

Ash cannot be judged
Judgment comes from anger
at not being where you want or need to be
If you wish to be judged
then judge

Bones and Ash

Bones and ash says clearly
in its own essence
that life is so much more
than the body
It does not end
with the bones and ash
of our being
It goes on and on

The Ash of Time

My Billy love
who can know more than you
at this moment of the sacred ash?
For after all is said and done
the ash survives all things in form
The body becomes old and worn
yet the ash is fresh each lifetime
It can never grow old
only bold in its newness
The ash, the ash
My River is the ash of time

The Cremation Ground

The cremation ground makes a space
for everyone's bones and ash
The ash blows in Vayu's wind
and settles on life about to come
The bones remain as a reminder
of death's union with life

My Life

My life is the ash I wear on my being
for you, chela

The Ash of the Cremation Grounds

The ash of the cremation grounds
fits my being like a tight glove
I wear the ash
as a Shaivite
a Shaivite turned loose
to run past the burning
tantric fires of time

With my hair blowing
in the aftermath of Vayu's breath
I run free
amongst the bony ash
of all dead thoughts
forever being born
again and again

Stillness must come to the mind
for the heat of the burning embers to be felt
When the mind is not stilled
all is lost in the wind
and the ash is scattered everywhere
Control the ash
and you control your life

The Path

The Way to God

Only children aren't afraid
of being alone
They learn
to play games
by themselves
As they grow
they begin to feel
I must do this, I must do that
Pressure builds up
and they forget to be light
They become as heavy
as all the burdens
they are forced to carry

Guru says,
Give me your burdens
to hold for a while

Chela becomes lighter
then stronger
Little by little
he is able to hold his own
and that which was a burden
doesn't seem so heavy

The way to God
is by the strength one is taught
at the feet of devotion
The bhakta learns quickly
while loving the Mother

The Heart's Path

When you make
the conscious choice to surrender
the path becomes your joy

The drink I drink
comes from the depths of the Ganga

I crave no possessions
As a yogi
I sit on the seat of compassion
I suffer no pain
from the want of the senses

I have practiced
the heart's path forever

All of this
I give to you, chela
to enjoy, to learn
to have, to keep

I Bow Down

I bow down to all that is holy

My father is Shiva
My mother is Kali
And I am the freedom of both

My brother is called kindness
My sister is called compassion
My truth is called life
My child is called love
My friend is called wisdom
My aunt is called karma
My uncle is called dharma
My heart is called pure
My mind is called virtue
My chela is called my own

The Essence of Wonder

The pure intellect
must be constantly sought after
The crust of man's ego
must be dug away
by the fires of Kali's eyes
If a man is to find his own purity
he must first arm himself
with his own joy
and sense of humor

If my chelas can learn
to greet each moment
the way they greet their Ma
they will have the essence of wonder
in their lives

Flowers on the Path

I try to put fresh flowers
on the path before them
so they can feel the soft scent
of life on their feet
Sometimes a thorn
is left on the path
and they bleed

Awareness

Do you know I love you
just the way you are?
Do you know you are perfect
in your Mother's eyes?

If you want to change
the change must come
from the perfection of now
The ego says you are not nice
the way you are
But the ego only speaks like that
so you get upset and can't change

Do you understand, my chelas?
They call me Ma, they call me Guru
but I am nothing without my chela's hand in mine
Your hand is perfect now as it is
Just know this
and let's get on with our lives
one foot in front of the other

This is not an easy teaching
this teaching by the cremation ground
If you go too fast
you will be burnt without knowing why

If you go too slow
you will not burn at all
and that is the worst possible thing
Let your lusts and desires die now
Come dead into my arms
and we will walk into the flame together

Suddenly and magically
you and the Mother
are one in the ash
one in the flame
one in the flesh

You are the rose in my garden
that I must place the thorns in
Yet I show you where to step
not to get pricked

I teach you awareness
Don't be afraid to smell the lovely rose
as long as you are aware of the thorns
Thorns can be attachment—
laziness, righteousness
or simply lack of courage
I shall give you my courage
to go toward the flame
at the pace I allow you to go

Discrimination

Discrimination is the essence of the third sight
born from awareness
and the four-cornered heart
Discrimination is born from awareness
Without awareness
discrimination will die
Yet awareness is nothing without the third eye
You learn this when you forget
the me, the my, and the I

I dance only with death
leaving awareness to find her mate
Discrimination is the Father of God
Look to each corner
before you choose your moment to be complete
For without the Father of God
you can never find the Mother's feet
Awareness is only the first step
It must mate with discrimination
for the tantric fate to be complete

Love what you have
and you will love what you cannot see
That is awareness of the soul
and the beginning of the four-cornered heart

The way of the heart
is the four-cornered path
Look and see
if you can close your eyes into infinity

The Root of Karma

The root of karma
is false neediness
The grabbing on to emotions
will not allow you to feel
the deeper love of what is before you
Let go all things
of the mind

The Dance

You ask: *Will I ever learn
all there is to learn?*
I answer: *You already know*

The dance only goes on
because you have forgotten the steps

Every minute of the day
you must know
in your soul of souls
that you have done all this before
before time was able to be counted

Come gently into my arms
We all wait for the dance to begin

River / Fire Darshan

When you sit by my River
facing the dhuni
the flame allows you
to see glimpses of your complete soul
The smoke of the dhuni
invites the gods and goddesses
to play at the water's edge
with the child inside every chela

In that moment
of Ganga and Agni
the chela's mind stops
and when the mind stops
sorrow stops, too

Just sit quietly by the fire
Let it burn your mind
into submission
to yourself

The Butterfly

The freedom in the butterfly's wings
Such a fragile thing
She can fly free in the wind
yet the slightest breeze
can throw her off a branch
if she is not careful

She cares not
for the judgment of others
or the minds of some
for she is complete inside herself
and can fly without her wings
to other times and other places
But she chooses to remain close
to where she can be seen by her children

If you hold out your hand
she will fly onto your fingers
and let you see gently
into her heart
For she is the butterfly called life
that death so enjoys
She is light of heart
and filled with love for all things
Though fragile, she is strong

Can her wings break from the winds of the mind
or is she so light
the winds pay her no mind?

The Lotus of the Quiet Mind

To know oneself completely
is to know the higher wisdom
of the heart
To die when one is alive
is to live fully
letting no mind bring you
into the hells of time
Only timelessness
can bring you joy

Mother Earth, who collects your ash
protects you against yourself
Blessed are those who find her in that moment
before physical death called life
Uncloud your mind and enjoy the moment
Drink the wine of time
Uncloud the senses

I am longing
for your growing unconsciousness
Your ability to change is in your hands
Cell by cell, change can come to all of you
The sky of the brain
can be reached with humility
One who lives with his ego
cannot love the moment
A lotus grows in the quiet
the stem in the dark mud of chaos
Clean yourself of your self
and become the lotus of the quiet mind

A Man Free

If you die
when you are alive
you are free of the senses
the desire to want all things
for only the top layer of pleasure
disappears in a haze of smoke

A man free
is a form of God
not distant
but here
in the now

Solace

The solace of each other's love
is the way of the path
the path that leaves us naked and young

Why Pretend to Love

Why pretend to love
when your love is so real?
I wear the ash
to make a path for you
to follow me in the darkness of night
into the brightness of soul

The Path of Fallen Ash

My Baba stares at the world
through the ash on his face
As he laughs or cries
the ash makes a path
that is easy for you to follow
He encourages the mind to die
in the pursuit of God's love

When you are eager to meet God
as a lover, father, mother, child,
the fallen ash will show you the way

When God asks,
Servant, why do you seek me?
You must bow low and say,
I am you
and I must find this out fully in this life
He shall meet you
on the path of fallen ash

Whether you are in the temple
or singing in your room
God can hear and see you so clearly
You are never alone
for the breath of breath is always in your heart

To feel yourself alive is to feel God

Love

Love is the Reason

Love is not a feeling to be taken lightly
Love is trying not to hurt another person
but listening to the Mother's word
Love is trying not to dominate each other
Love is the strongest feeling known to man
an all encompassing passion
stronger than Shiva's trident
Everyone wants to feel the Mother's love
You can feel it in each other
if you can become the Mother

Love is the reason for love
Love is to be cherished
Love can help you shed the world
Love is a flower
opening up the petals of your life
Love creates life's flow
Love lets you hold the trident
and let go

Love is as old
as the womb of time
Love remembers times and places
and calls upon today
to say, *I love you*

Without love
there would be an empty, barren womb

Love is all you need to lay your head on
that same breast
And drink to your heart's content

Love is what is deathless in you
that which cannot die at death
Love is not your body that decays
and grows old with yesterday's karma
and fear of tomorrow's death
Love is like the oil that burns
in my puja lamps
Love is a monkey
that was once a God
Love is Shiva

Love is the wind
that cannot be caught
but can be felt

Love as a Razor

I have only one path to teach
and that path is love

I use love as a razor
to scrape away the scars
left over from ego's wars
against the heart

The Core of Love

I can bring you
to the heart of the self
and you will know without a doubt
the core of love

A child has this love
in the core of his being
A child has unconditional love
He knows only how to wrap
his arms around you
and exclaim, *I love you*

Every human being
has that inner child in himself
hidden deep in the hidden self
If you ask the hidden child his name
he will answer,
My name is love

And You Will Know Love

Love is listening
to my River Song
and thinking
This is about today
this is the bounty of the most high
Love always lives, never dies

Love is always giving, never asking
Love is never saying anything ugly or untrue

Love is saying God is everything
and knowing you are part of that God

Love is being abundant, kind, and generous
Love is trusting

Love is the heart of the Mother
that takes away the loneliness
of the human condition

Love is yesterday's lovers
turning into today's friends

Love never begins and never ends
But goes on
lifetime after lifetime
starting again where you left off

And you will know love that won't disappear

The Face of Love

The one song that is sung in harmony
with all the heavens and earth
is the song of love
When I teach in the moment of awareness
the silent song of love drips from my lips
in perfect time with my chela's breath

Love does not look to hurt
Love does not look to crucify
Love is the godlike substance
that heals and soothes

Your time cannot be possessed
It can only flow through your fingers
touching ever so lightly the heart of awareness

When there is anger
it will disappear in the face of love
When there is pain
that too will leave in the face of love
When the burden of life
falls upon your shoulders
just think of an invisible force
helping you carry that burden
to the River

The River is ever so grateful
for all that is given to Her
even your pain is a gift to the Mother Ganga
when you place it at her feet

The River

My River

My River is a golden one
It flows gently, caressing, touching everyone
My River is not understood by all
But chela, don't worry
Rivers don't need to be understood
Just sit by them

My River is not far away from me
always flowing into my heart
My River has never asked to be worthy of my love
It just is, it just was, it just will be

My River is tender, my River is harsh
My River eases the burning inside a mother's heart
My River is the Ganges, the Ganga, my home
The River that makes a peasant a king
The River that gives any child a throne

When I look toward my River
and see sadhus worshipping the Giver
and see children playing upon its banks and
splashing in the River
and see temples shining in all their glory
and cities so old they can write their own story
I bow to that River

As men long to die by this River
and widows shed tears as they cry by the River
I give one long sigh by my River Ganga, Gangé

Those who sit silently
watching the children play
find that the River flows every which way
into the darkness, into the light
My River has black pearls upon her breast at night
The eyes of the Guru watch in delight
as all its streams turn darkness into light

So you see this River is me
And I am she who bows in ecstasy to the River
to the sound of Krishna playing His flute
to the gopis dancing by Her sister, the Yamuna
to the sannyasin yearning and learning
to the child singing a song of bliss of God
to the young bride who kissed her God

The River gently flows into the heart of all
making no distinction

Children Play by my River

Children play by my River
Sadhus stay by my River
Temples gold by my River
Cities old by my River
Old men die by my River
Widows cry by my River

Bright lights reflect upon my River
Starry nights hang above my River
My Guru wears a blanket by my River
My Guru, the Giver of the River

The River doesn't know who sits before Her
For all who come to hear Her, bow and adore Her
Here is what it feels like to be by the River
To sit in the gentleness of God's breath
My River has the Wind God bowing
to Her gentle ripplings along the banks of life
My River has Kali dancing by Her cremation grounds
all through the night

My River is so very precious I claim Her as my own
My River is Kashi, My River, my own

I sat by my River eons ago
I sit by my River and tell the story you all surely know
A child dances and runs and feels the ecstasy
of God by that River

And the River flows into every child's heart
The River is filled with ashes of the dead
Yet the River has newness of Her own
and takes away pain, bringing joy instead

The River is complete, the River is you
Most of all it is by the River that we meet

River Chela

Come see what I am
my River chela
Come see into the River of my heart

The River and the Sand

The River and the sand
share the same wave
Where is the difference?
In the mind of man

Man separates
God puts together

The Ganga

The sleeping baby
is like the Ganga
at Her quiet moments
She sleeps sweetly
and all is well on Her banks

The Ganga awakens
at the sound of children playing
in Her waters
She becomes alert
for She is the Mother
and must forego all sleep
to protect Her young
She watches Her children, and sighs

One day they will have grown-up minds
and forget their gentle sleep
The guru will remind them not to

To Live at My River

Awaken my children
Open your eyes
Let yourselves abandon your thoughts
of power, jealousy and hate
Awaken my chelas
there is a far greater way to live at my River
than just hearing of it
There is a way to be it

Where Do the Dead Play?

I say to my chelas
Live beyond the world
yet don't be afraid to touch it

I tossed my heart into the Ganges
while my chelas watched in amazement
Like a child I danced and played
everywhere her waters could be found

Your soul knows how to play
and it longs to feel the wind
Are you a servant of your mind
or can you find the blowing wind within?

If the world is for the living
where do the dead play?
They play among our children
protecting their every breath
They watch us love
and they say, "Subek"
All is the same in life as in Death

Do you think once dead the soul is lost?
Nay, it still follows the Mother's way
You cannot shake off Death with a sigh

Death should be played with or Death will die
For Death's memories live on

The River's Song

The River Goddess
teaches you of sadhus staying by my River
watching the children playing by my River
The children swim in the Mother's womb
in delight of the pure moment

Men die by my River
Widows cry by my River
yet the River takes your heaviest burden
and puts it on Her breast
The River does not test
She just is

The more you remove the world
the more you receive the River

Ether, air, fire, water, and earth
all bow to the River Child's birth
The placenta is formed in graveyards past
for life is always moving
like the River
But life does not last

The River's words are true and deep
She sings in the world's subtle sleep

I am, I am, I am
sings the River's song
I am existence
I am love

There is no trace of thought in the River Child
She is at peace with the River's edge
She is wild
She runs naked in the wind

Son of the Wind God, my Baba
The River of my heart exists for you
to bless my chelas with
There is nothing except God's River
All else has no meaning
All else is illusion

River, they are thirsty
Quench their thirst
Take my chelas into your deepest part
Let them drown in your nectar

River, your watery grave is my home
My ashes will not spill alone
They meet with all those
the River has taken home

Children play with my ash
Sadhu, where do you stray with my ash?
Widows, how can you cry
with my ash near your eyes?
Young men cannot die wearing my ash
Cows stray all the day
stepping upon the sacred ash
I will always wear the ash

Come to My River

It is unwise to wander aimlessly from life to life
without absorbing the moment on the path now
Look around you, chela, and soak in my Ganga
The River never compromises your purity

Children come play by my River
I, your Ma, sit in bliss
all the day by my River
The River of my heart is as clear as spotless glass

Come to my River; it is all I ask
The River path has obstacles
which the River herself will remove
with her flowing waters and father's wind
Come to my River and look deep within
My River has so many stories
that have never been told

What possessions could you possibly bring
to the River's edge
when her temples of gold
are worshipped by the dead?

The River Ganga is deeper
than any ocean, near or far
Our River is what I am and what you are

In Her River
the Mother wears Her ash
and no one asks why

The Waters of the Ganga

No soul is lost
who touches the waters
of the Ganga

No soul is lost
who feeds from her breasts
always full

The corpse of life
loses its desire for worldly things
and turns to God
for sustenance

Baba

My Baba

Once my Laxman shaved his head
I was so mad
I asked why
He answered,
So the children can see all of me
He then removed his longoti
and ran naked with the young
All fear of life left the children
They were free in their youth

I do not know what manner of God
this crazy man is
and I don't care
He is mine, shaved hair or long hair or jetta
naked or dressed
He is mine, without judgment
I run by his side
with his flesh touching my own
or with only a shadow of last life's ash

I have enough of my Baba
never to be lonely upon this earth
My Baba thinks thoughts of sunlight
upon the flowers
as he teaches his Ma to teach

You are going right up to the doors of death this life
are you not, my love? he asks his Ma
I answer, *I have already taken*
the live ones through them, my Lord

Baba Is Everywhere

In the early days my Baba used to say to Ma
Do not despair
your Baba is everywhere
always here, always there

My Baba would say,
Laugh, Ma, never forget to laugh and play
even when your heart is ripped out
So I do, my chelas

Catch Time

My Baba says
Catch time, Ma, in a net of love
and let it go slowly, controlling time with love

Time, time
The wandering child must be brought
to his Mother's ashen feet
so Kali has a meal to eat
Time, time
says his dark, blue Mother
Slow down your breath
or the Mother will hunger

The secret of time
is not to waste any of it
and then to waste it all
at your Mother's feet

Only Baba Is Now

You must become as a child
a child who loves to watch
the wide river's flow
a child who knows for sure
the Mother loves him

Or you must become like the corpse
lying quiet in the cemetery of time
doing nothing and having no worries
like a heavy stone
thrown into the Ganga
just going without a mind
where the River takes you
or like words
without paper to put them down on

So free
without companions of mind or culture
Seek the divine truth within the corpse
Words and sayings are illusions
of a moment that has passed

Only Baba is now
Birth and death
are both illusions

Only Baba is now
The common mind is misleading
There is no hunger in the corpse
There is no desire in the dead
There is no judgment
in the cremation grounds—
only bones and ash
Do not the vultures eat the flesh
and dine on the heart of man?
What use does this body have for us
if it's placed at the wrong place in life?
Samadhi exists only at the feet of the Mother

Observe the dead
There you will learn compassion
There you will learn trust
There you will learn to be generous

Laxman

To me, Laxman
the thing that matters
besides their love
is their stillness

I think it has to be
a personal decision
to use Baba and Ma
as a way to happiness

We are here for that reason
Make the right decision

I Play with God

I walk with God
and God talks with me
I talk to God
and God listens to me
I play with God
and God plays with me
Then Baba says he is tired

In Your Joy of Sadness

Once I said to Laxman,
I am unhappy without you
Boy, did he get mad at me

He said,
I am the trees that shade you
I am the sun that warms you
I am the scent of the flowers you love to smell
I am the moon in the darkest night
I am the storms that shine in the blue sky
I am the oceans, the rivers
How can you be sad
when you have all these things?

I bowed my head low
and said with tears in my eyes,
I am so unhappy without you

He laughed and said,
It is the flesh of the Guru
that tastes the sweetest of all
It is good to desire Guru's flesh
as long as you feed everyone
in your joy of sadness

Ma

To Feed Everyone

Each step I took
on my journey toward you, chela
was filled with uncertainty
but also filled with trust
Trust that Baba was and is love incarnate
and that I, his consort
would always have full breasts
to feed everyone

Baba, Always Keep Me Full

I can be in the tunnel of dark deaths
and rotted thoughts
for I carry his warmth on my breath
Naught can claim my abundance
unless I want to give it away
Therefore I do not hoard my love
but let it flow
not unlike my gracious River

Baba, always keep me full
so I can show the dark places of their minds
and teach them not to fear
the opposite thoughts of light
thoughts that come not only from this
but from all lifetimes merged into the moment
The pattern of life
has to be worked out in the moment
and the old threads must be removed
with the skill of a surgeon

Choose the Now

When I went into the spring fields of death
to choose life for my form, this life
I chose the now
when we could all be together upon this earth
to swim in the Ganga of life
as Mother and child

Learn in the Waters of Now

You have been touched by my love
and now chela, you wait for Ma
to untangle your lives even more than before
The difference now is that you have the ability
to climb out of yourself and become strong
in your love for your Ma

You all dream of tomorrow
when today has just begun
If you can learn in the waters of now
we will be able to swim together
in tomorrow's light

Press the dead flowers to your heart
but do not forget the scent
of the fresh moment of now

Come Play with Your Ma

Oh, my chelas
the Mother wears so many faces
each of them as real as the next
Our lives are the fulfillment
of all the timeless places
I have taken you in darshan

The void you seek
is the void you are
I want to give you me so badly
I can taste it

Drop what you do not need
I am waiting for you
Come play with your Ma
as the gopis did with Krishna

My table is always set
Come share my meal
We will feast on his bounty
and enjoy his daily bread
of love, hugs, and kisses
Too simple, you may say
Why do you want to complicate God?

You can sit on a high plateau
but how will you know of Earth's Mother
if you are freezing in the snow?
You can hide in a jungle tree
but how will you know of the mountains?
You may grow jetta and hide away
but how will you learn of my River?
You may escape in an old temple forever
but how will you hear the children's laughter?

Come sing my song, chela
Make it your own
Come walk along the banks of the Ganga
with Ma
I will teach you
of mountains, jungles, temples, rivers,
nagas, Gods, babas, swamis,
oceans, trees, monkeys, and me

In a whirlwind of love
I will give you calmness on earth
I will sing to you of burning ghats
and Kali's nighttime glory

Hold Tight to Your Ma's Feet

If my chelas can learn
to greet each moment
the way they greet their Ma
they will have the essence of wonder
in their lives

If I hold each moment of life
like I hold His feet to my breast
the moment becomes large
for what can be small
when one holds on to the Guru's feet?

Even if you make mistakes
hold tight to your Ma's feet
If you could find a protectiveness
in the feet of the Guru
you would be able to value your own being
knowing that even as you hear your mind
running fast along the track of life
you still have her feet to go to
in time of need or wrong action

When the tears fall upon the ground
in my hour of mourning for humanity's needs
I always remember that my Baba loves me
and my chelas love me
I am one blessed woman
and you, my chelas are blessed people
Know this and begin to live through
your mistakes as lessons in life

With You

With my chela's love
I am ready for anything
Without you
I am just a woman loving God
With you
I have many hands to work with
many faces to smile with
With you
we can feed everyone
as our Baba says

I Give Everything Away

I give every child my full heart
I hold back nothing
I give everything away
every moment of my life
I ask for nothing in return
I love freely
everyone who crosses my path
I only know how to love
not to hate
no matter what is done to me

It is the way
my Baba taught me
in the cremation grounds of life
and for that I touch his feet
always

Separation of Flesh

When my chela asks,
Ma, how do I get close to you?
I simply reply,
You already are
But you have to drop
the proudness of lifetimes
and gain the humility
of just being happy
at the Mother's feet
yet always asking for more
Demand from me your individuality
at my feet
as I busy myself
placing flowers at his

My separation of flesh
from my Baba
is for you, chela
to understand that sometimes
I too am lost
carrying this burden of flesh
without his own
to be seen by your eyes

Yet I know
I can swim by myself
surrounded by all of you
in my Ganga's journey
back home to death

Guru

Accept the Feet of the Guru

To accept the feet of the Guru
in one's heart
is to begin to live a full life
Once the Guru has received the chela
everything unknown becomes known
or at least all that needs to be known
becomes known

The Guru picks you up
from the dark, infinite abyss
and brings you light in your life
Alone no more
the voyage becomes exciting
Once filled with foreboding
the chela now walks proudly
without pride on all paths
holding the hand of the Guru

To heal the scars of life
the Guru purges the chela's gloom
and says,
You are safe my sons, my daughters
safe in my arms

The River of the Guru's Love

In the infinite ocean
of the self
as the mind is stilled
the chela finds a place in his heart
to fit the River of the Guru's love

This River
touches all the Gods
as Ganesh removes the obstacles
in the River's way
The River is the source
of the Stilled Mind
She refreshes the soul
and makes it moist again
Dryness of the world
stops completely
and the dew
of the Mother's love
allows the River easy access
to the chela's heart of hearts,
the Guru

The River
is the Baba's source of love
and the Mother's source of surrender

Guru and Chela

When I was young
on this path, this life
the thing I treasured most
was the intimacy of Guru and chela

I vowed always
to keep this going
as I handed down all
that was given me

When my Baba spoke on death
I listened very carefully
The word became the Guru
the Guru became the word
When I hear his words on death
I, the chela, know I must teach
his words in life

Chela, practice
the words of the Guru
Give your attention
to all she has to say
She does not need words
yet she speaks for you
to absorb her flesh
in your own learning
of the truth of tantric passion

He who is with Guru
can see life through dead eyes
eyes that cannot see desires of flesh

only the desires of the heart
bound hand and foot to the soul

The soul is simply hidden
in the karma that surrounds it
lifetime after lifetime
By itself it is perfect
Cluttered by mind values
it escapes the form of perfection
by the ego that will become master
if the mind does not die
by Guru's hand
slain by Kali and burned on the pyres
closest to the Mother Ganga's pyre

Before anything existed
there was time
the movement of space

Place chela and guru in the same place
at the same time
darshan is formed
It does not matter what is said
only what is heard
Darshan is food for the chela's soul
The meaning of darshan
is the blessing of the Guru
When you can sit in this space of two
you receive the blessing for you and you alone
It becomes very intimate

I Am The Now

Neither childhood, youth, nor old age
can make a dent in the soul's way
or conception of life
As one flows into the other
it can be a choppy transition
or an even movement

The Guru comes along
to show chela that the passage of life's moments
is the same as death
Every second a little death occurs
as time buries the past
and looks in the present
for yesterday's answers

The Guru says,
I am the now
Use me this moment so I do not bend
with the burden of my own truth
held at bay for you, chela
In the past, present, and future
I remain the same

The Guru has nothing to do with your eyes
only your heart

I, the Guru, laugh when life is pleasant
and weep when it is painful

When the Guru
is in the formless moment
neither pleasant nor painful exists—
only the supreme godhead, Baba

When chela becomes trapped
in the illusion of opposites
like beauty and ugliness
the Guru says,
Close the eyes of judgment
and see only God
in his many forms of humanity
and judge not lest you be judged

And this is how you can bring karma to others
by forcing them, with a fragile mind
to judge back in defense

God has no defenses
He does not need any

Ashen Tears

When chela's flesh
gives way to bones and ash
the Guru cries ashen tears
that fill the Ganga
with her grief

She wears the ash
upon her breast

The Mother

The Mother (as Sun Goddess)

The Mother in all her forms
caresses her chelas
while she consumes the sun
inside her being
Every part of herself
brings light to all places
The ego is consumed by her brightness
and dies without battle or fight
She has been eating the sun
since the beginning of time

Love the Mother

When the heart aches, love the Mother
more passionately than ever before
Let the Guru feed the hungry heart
with her full breasts
Put yourself quietly to one side
and caress nature's truth of loving the Earth Mother
The prana around you becomes soaked
with this passion for love
to fill the hungry heart

Through the Eyes of the Mother

When you can see
through the eyes of the Mother
you will see your beauty

All that is
is inside the chela's soul

If you take what the Mother gives
you can feel your own beauty

Drink Deeply

In the silent preserves of the Mother's love
you can feel her essence
if you still your mind
Even beyond life
there is life in her essence

The Mother fills you with life
Like a child
you can sing
and love and play
all in her presence
She will guide you
out of the darkest day
and teach you that your soul
is the heart of God

When darkness is upon you
the Mother brings forth the light
As she raises her hand the sun listens
She gathers your soul in one hug
her body near your own
You find she is not unlike yourself
The waters mirror her light
for she is one with all light

Hold her tight
If you drink deeply of her cup
you will see your life void of misery
Raise this cup high above your head
Offer it to the gods
Then drink your fill
your cup of joy
in your Mother's dance
You do not drink alone
You drink with the Mother's lips
Drink deeply
The liquid never disappears
In life as in death
In death as in life
Drink your fill of the Mother

She will be your company until death
and then she takes another form
She walks into the garden of the valley
and you will smell her fragrance as never before
You will wait with her at death
until another life's dawn

Hymn to the Mother

I have wronged you, Mother
I committed a sacrilege
and my sacrilege was lust

I have wronged you, Mother
I committed a sacrilege
and my sacrilege was loneliness

I stood by the Well of Infinity and forgot
Forgot that the water runs deep
I who leave, who stood by the ocean
forgot the depth of the ocean

I who leave
who witnessed the sky
in the early morn with the sun ablaze
forgot the sun
I who set my eyes
upon a star
forgot how the star can shine

I have wronged you, Mother
and made you weak
For I, your son
forgot to love myself

I began to seek
outside my own being
a lesser truth

And yet in your moments of compassion
You forgive my sins
For I am but a humble man
petty in many ways
jealous in even more ways

Yet one thing I never denied, my Mother
my Mother Durga
I never denied your love
I only forgot

I have wronged you, Mother
and in so doing
I lost myself
in a world with no meaning

I have wronged you, Mother
and tears now fall upon the Earth
as I touch your feet
and beg forgiveness
from one who always forgives

The Sun Necklace

They say in Hindu scriptures
the sun was always hung
in the universal way of things
around the Mother's neck
As she hungered each day
she consumed the sun
bringing darkness of night
upon Earth, her daughter
As time passed, the Goddess
wanted her ornament back
and her sun necklace was renewed
day after day after day

I hunger to eat the sun
and all she takes on
for the sun
is the greatest cremation ground of all

How Do You Partake of the Meal Set by the Mother?

How do I partake of the meal set for me
by the Mother?
With a want so deep
that all thoughts are beaten down

The soul is then emptied
and hungry for stimulation
The food looks so appetizing
and the chela is so empty
that he comes in the mindless state of the child
hungry to eat
from the Mother's table

He whose mind is full
has no room
to enjoy the food of life
she has prepared

Play at the Mother's Feet

Pride and ignorance
will keep you from learning how to play
at the Mother's feet

All things you hold on to
will bring you pain
hour after hour
When your hands are empty
there is nothing to hold you down
Possessions are beauty of the mind
Wealth and belongings
live only a short time

But love for the Mother
goes on and on

He who feels his mind running wild
cannot feel the wind
running through his hair
What is the mind?
Only despair

I Am There

The chela calls out
by the hungry flame:
You do not come, my Mother
and I wait by the fiery dhuni
yet everywhere is the same
I walk by the Ganga
and cannot feel you, my Mother
Why are you avoiding me?

My child, my child.
I am the smoke from the dhuni
Look close at the fire
I am there
Look close at the waters of the River
and you will feel my sweet wetness on your flesh
In the mountain
I am there

I can hear your sorrow
I can feel your pain
I am your Mother
You are not looking hard enough for me

Do you have any idea how long a night can last
when you do not look inside yourself
for the Mother?

You will see me
I am alive inside of you
Do not wilt with longing
I am with you

Children

Once a Child Claims You

Once a child claims you
you are a prisoner for life
Children steal your hearts
with their simplicity and pureness
Children who play in my River
stay with her wetness
all the day

My Ganga flows ever so gently
to the waiting children of her River

Shiva, the embodiment of Godhead
stops Maya, his consort
in order for the children to know him
He says to the youth of the Ganga
From the unreal, my child
I will lead you into the light of the real

Maya laughs for she knows the child must grow up
in an adult's mind
and she will be waiting

Mother Ganga is the refuge of all children
Never has this Mother turned a child away
Her love will embrace the young forever and ever
She accepts those all others reject

Youth rejoices in her presence
Her age matters not
Her heart is forever young

You must grow and know each child as your own
Your own youth's tragedies will disappear

How strangely different youth is from middle age
as you place your hand on a child's heart
Yet the old become young again
Only the soul remains old
even in the beauty of youth

If you sit for hours before your puja
it would not be as sacred
as a child's smile
coming from his eyes and heart

Only the Self is Real

The children, the children
my babies can give so much
to those who will come after them
simply because they have been given so much
They trust fully
for they trust in themselves

Be aware, children
the River flowing in your youth
is the same River that will flow in your old age
The River God never changes
Only he who sits before it
If you merge within the River
you will become the River flow
and when this body falls from your soul
time will make a new house
for your never-changing perfect spirit

What does not bloom
does not die
The ever-changing body
is perishable
Only the self is real
All else is but an illusion

The Children at Connor's Nursery

Little children
what beautiful smiles upon your faces
You welcome each moment
without questioning
Why do I have AIDS?

If we all lived in that place
of no whys
we could go on
and enjoy the breath
we were given, given by a force
higher than ourselves
as you know yourself to be

The breath must be measured
and by controlling it with your mind
you become the complete
master of your destiny

Come Little Children

Come little children
to my waiting arms
I am the Ganga
I am the River
I am the Giver

Hug the Children

When one receives
what one needs
his wants become smaller and smaller

Hug the children
You will give them
what they need
Even if they say *No*
they will feel good in their hearts

A Child's World

Equal to God
and the fruit of the Mother
The chela lives
in a child's world

Only in the Moment

Restless is the mind
of a grown man

The child lives
only in the moment

The Moment

Between His Mother's Breasts

Grow in the moment
where the past and future
have no name
Seek nothing from time
only his Mother's name
Spill not Shakti
on worldly thoughts
Ask time for a place
between his Mother's breasts
to lay your head softly and rest

To Live in Ma's Moment

In this garden called life
where flowers bloom on paths to nowhere
and weeds grow in the form of disease and pain
the Mother lights the road
with her brightness
and says to chela:
Take my hand
I will show you
where the thorns lie in wait
for the soft flesh of your feet

She warns you of greed and jealousy
The ego balks at her teaching
yet your heart knows her words are true

For the sake of a moment's pleasure
so many are consumed with a passion
for more of what they do not need
The Mother strips the ego of desire
and says to chela:
Take what you want from the world
Do not let the world rule you
Then you can serve, dance, and play
and feed everyone a cookie, a smile, a touch
It is all yours
The good and the bad merge
into the same moment of detachment
Only the soul exists
and you begin to live in Ma's moment

Will You Follow Me?

Your subtle sleep comes forth
and awakens your whole being
to the moment
All that you have learned
in moments or lives past
comes into play
in the now

The Guru then says:
If I follow my Baba,
will you follow me?

Can I leave you for a split second in eternity
to be with my Baba
in my simplicity of no flesh
Will you follow your heart
and know that you, too
can control your moment
and become like the child bride, Bhagavati
following her Laxman anywhere

If I climb the highest mountain
will you let me be?
If I grow my hair in jetta
will you care?

Will you care for Ma
as I play in the jungles?
That is what this poem means
Can you count on yourselves
to live in my moment?

If I go to the Ganga, will you be there?
Are you ready to dive into the waters
that purify the flesh and soul
and kill the ego?
Then swim in the milky white waters of my Ganga

If I go to my Swami, will you hear?
Will you heed the words of the timeless one?
Are you ready, my chelas?

If I follow my Baba, will you follow me?
If I climb the highest mountains
will you let me be?

If I swim in the sacred ash with death everywhere
will you follow the ash that falls from my hair?
Will you go to Rishikesh
and feed the lepers who live there?

If I follow my Baba, will you follow me?
Will you ask to be born of Kali's womb
resting in it between death and life
seeing no difference
between day and night?
For Kali is the Mother of time—
therefore the timeless one

Service

Hanuman

Hanuman, my Lord of Service,
I bow with my whole being
to your lotus feet
May I always walk in your shadow
of love and devotion
The Son of the Wind God
Watch over my chelas' hearts

Service

A heart cannot be full one moment
and skimpy the next
The mind controls when the body is lazy
The mind stops when service is done

So Simple

If you can give your heart only once
the path of service and love
becomes so simple

A Need to Serve

To slumber on this Earth
when there is such a need to serve
is truly a sad thing

The Promise of Hanuman

In our strength of being together
we will confound the world
with our love of service
True is the promise of Hanuman
to teach those
who vow to love
all who need love

Bow Tenderly to the Moment

It does not matter
what you do with your flesh in the day
as long as you give every moment its due
Whether you are doctors
nurses, teachers, house cleaners—
each moment must be an act of service
service that bows tenderly
to the moment

His Eyes Are Always Upon You

Hanuman's universe is perfect
His compassion awes the mind
Hanuman's truth is subtle
so subtle you can hardly see it
Clearly Hanuman's compassion is fathomless
It refreshes the Soul

Hanuman's love is absolute,
lighting up the soul
More precious
than the finest jewelry
Sweeter than the honey cup
The Mother helps you become aware
of the nature of the Monkey's love

If you can still the mind
you will feel Hanuman's eyes
always upon you
The Mother teases you
with her lila of illusion
Learn to dance with her heart
and you will be playing
with the Monkey's tail

The Greatest Teaching

Look deeply into the face
of her who wears the ash
There is nothing there
There is only a place
for you to look upon
like the shadow of the setting sun

She bows
for you and to you
to teach you humility
the greatest teaching of them all—
Humility

Continually
your body begins to rot
but your soul can live
and swim in the sea of humility
Never can you escape
the fingers of death
But you can learn
to hold Death's hand
and befriend Yama
the Lord of Death
in the Tibetan teaching
of the dead hand

Christ

At the Feet of Jesus

When my Christ came to me
my whole life changed
What used to matter
had little or no meaning
at the feet of Jesus

I made the conscious decision
to dedicate my life to service
after getting rid of my fear
of seeing Christ
in my living room

Kali Answers Only to Love

Kali answers only to love
and does not look at the long or short
of man's limit in time spaces
She gathers her seeds
that care nothing for cloths
made of sun or moon

Her children do not judge time
by the awakened sun
or the sleeping moon
Time ceases to be
and all becomes
the moment of human contact
with the divinity of timeless consciousness

Only in the moving fire
of the death place
in man's heart
can you place the garland of time
at the feet of the black night
called Kali Ma
The sun then rises between her toes
and her chelas march through life
with the scent of the Mother's feet
always upon them

She Lives to Free Your Soul

The stoic manner in which Kali comes to you
is her detachment from all form
even your own
She lives to free your soul
from the ego's clutches
She spares no ego
until the last piece of pride
is fried upon her spit
that turns over her hot fire

The truth cannot be hidden
You are not your ego
You are the higher self

When the Ego Dies

As rivers break down mountains
so Kali breaks down the ego
She is patient as the flowing River
going over and over the same dark spot
until it becomes one with one

One does not lose
his personality
but takes on a clearer light
of understanding
when the ego dies

The ego is the pit of hell
bringing only attachment and pain
to the chela's life forces

One without ego
is free of attachment

Freedom is the union
of the soul with the Mother

Kali

All seasons renounce their order
when the Dark Mother approaches their moment
Flowers raise their heads
for Kali's nourishment
She spreads her fragrant jasmine
on the waters of time
as she bathes the nighttime dead away
She does water puja
with ash upon her face
She acknowledges life without a frown
She wears the ash
as she wears her own skin—
the ash of dead thoughts

She burns karma in her dhuni
as Shiva's consort
The flame dances
to her tune of dead thoughts
and she laughs shrilly
into night's blackness

Ego

As Your Ego Dies

Oh my chelas, I love you
even when I swing Kali's sword

I hurt for you
as your ego dies
yet I continue to strike at the ego's being
for my love is detached from ego's pain

The Ego's Disguise

When the ego comes in disguises
of other entities
there is a moment of defiance
on the part of the true heart
It does not last long

When the ego says, *I am the doer*
the heart space skips a beat
and all is not right inside yourself
Face life with an openness
and the ego will disappear
disguises and all

Illusions

Illusions are created by ego
as a substitute
for the God-like substance
inside of you

The Smoke that Covers the Truth

The illusion of the things
you think you want
can disappear in a moment
of clear thought
Clarity is a weapon
used by the gods
to defeat the ego
You fear what you cannot see

Yet if you clear the smoke
that covers the truth
of your own beauty
You will see the cremation ground
as a place to play
without the sorrows of flesh

The Candle of Awareness

The ego has no existence
of its own
It is like darkness
without a flame
It is only the absence of light

If you light the flame of awareness
you will chase the ego away
It will have no home
and you will be free of pain

You need not live your life
without a candle of awareness

That is what guru is all about—
bringing awareness
where there was only darkness
light into blackness

Do not spend your life
listening to your ego
Feed your souls
not your minds

Yama

Death Does Not Die

Mother
Shall I ask
for knowledge of Death
while I am still alive
or wait for Death to claim me
before I ask?

Mother
l am young
what need do I have
for Death's answers?

Child
your mind must not be deceived
that Death does not
exist in life
Death is the fulfillment
of life's dreams

I walk tall in my cloth of ash
Only my eyes
sparkle with life
for they are dead, too
dead to the desires
of the mind only

The mind's eye
can see clearly
The third eye is the third wish
The truth of Death
lies between the eyebrows

I speak of Death
so fully in our lives
His red palms always upward
showing us compassion and truth
for all creative things

My Baba's Death is life
life in the breast of his chelas
Life in Death
is always a glorious thing to behold
My Baba lives in me

Baba, your Death
is the living proof
that Death does not die

At Yama's Table

The law of the universe
is to love each moment of understanding
and to find out what you don't comprehend
with complete openness

If you are unready to die
how will you ever be ready to live?
I make ready to die
every moment of life

I set a place at Yama's table
and place a name card next to Baba's
I share the appetizer called life
with all of you
so the table, when you are ready
will not look strange
or foreign to your eyes

Death is a cozier place than most
When life is over
it is a faultless system
of universal love

Death, Do Not Be a Stranger

Oh, my Lord of Death
Who will serve you?
Who will put flowers at your feet?
Who will wipe your forehead
and not be afraid?

My Lord Yama
who will gather your stolen ashes
of lives gone by
and spread them
on their breasts?

Who will caress your heart, my Lord of Death?
Why, I will
of course I will

I will teach of your beauty
of your skull
of your boneless fingers
playing death's song
on the instrument of life

All men and women
should honor Death's deeds
and bow low before his door
before knocking
Death will answer only the humble

The arrogant he will tell
to come through the back way
and lock the door on all wisdom of life

Yama
None seek him
yet all shall know him
I have always danced
with Death's teachings on my lips
That's why I can enjoy the child

Death is quite simple
He is just there

Death's River, feel my tears
I am weeping for those
who do not fondle you in life
River, help me to teach about Death
so they can begin to live
unafraid of all things unknown

I live with Death's breath on my brow
I scream out,
Know him now
For what they see, they will not fear
and what they feel, they will cherish

Death
do not be a stranger to my children
for they are not afraid of the dark
Their Ma is always there

Come dance with my deathly partner
I welcome you, Yama, into my life
and the lives of my chelas
Come sweetly, my gracious lover
Be tender and slow in your love making

Take a full, long lifetime
to claim your bride and her children
Let them learn the steps of Death's dance
for a hundred years or more
Teach them every day of your tantric life
my beautiful Death

When death comes early
to those with AIDS
my children will be able to show them
the beauty of Death's journey
They will squeeze all they can
from the grapes of life
and squeeze Death, too
Death will say,
Good, you know me
I will not make you afraid

Live and Die with a Full Heart

I want you all strong
on this journey of ours
to the cremation grounds
so when you begin to feel
the hot ash beneath your feet
you won't blister
You will be able to enjoy the moment
knowing in no way are you attached
to the burning body
that used to house your soul
When you learn this
you become free to wander
the cremation grounds in life

When the body is spread out
on the hot, fiery wood
and flowers are placed
with incense around it
you will laugh in pleasure, not in fear
Fear kills so many moments in life
and steals death's fullness
before your very eyes
Gather up courage
like flowers in a field
and know your Ma
will help you live
with a full heart
and die with a fuller one

Subek

Is the wave different from the sea?
Is chela different from the Mother?
No, each is needed
to complement the other
Both are children
Both are the Mother

Are the clouds different
from the clouds and the sky?
No, one is part of the other
Is death different from life?
No, one lives inside the other

Fear cannot live
where there is understanding of life
Death does not bring dying
Only the mind
separates man from God
All is the same—
the flower and the scent
the Mother and the Child

Subek

The Skull

I Am the Skull

I am really the teaching of the Skull
I have no eyes that see the failing of man
I have no ears that hear his lies
I have no mouth to speak of all this
I simply am

I am the Skull
My skin is made to decay
I am stark, I am real
I cannot hurt
I cannot feel
I am just here
a skull-like figure
to take away your fear
of death and life
a Skull
whose heart has ceased to beat

I am the coldness that warms the heat
I am the Skull
called Man
Touch me and I live

Stripped Clean

When one surrenders
to the Guru's love
there is a very still mind that allows the chela
to weep real tears
and yet not be attached to anything

Emotion is stripped away
with Kali's flaying sword
and what is left is clean and pure

It is very frightening
to be stripped clean of all emotions
we have clung to for lifetimes
But what is left is a happy ending
All hearts are mended
All the world's cruelty is consumed and spit out
upon Mother Kali's burning ghats
The flesh falls away
and the Skull is left clean and bare

All of life becomes a joy
a celebration of purity
a cleansing of the soul
The Skull knows
The Skull hears
The Skull is free from attachment
The Skull is merely a child-like quality
of a child-like nature
never judging, always watching
as my Baba watches his Ma
in all things, big and small

The Skull knows it all
not through knowledge or wisdom
but just by being there
The Skull is truly the soul of man
and the hand of God
The Skull reaches out its blinded eyes
and sees all that is in motion
The Skull stops the motion of the mind
with its own power
The clarity comes from the dark Mother Tara
to whom I bow very low
Love will give birth to service
Service will give birth
to the space of the heart
You all can have what is yours to keep
the raw texture of the skull
If you want hard enough
then ask Kali to strip away
the ego from the bones of desire

Ask Kali
to spread your ashes of karma
on her body
to blend in the Ganga's waters
when she bathes

It is not so hard to be as the Skull of time
There is no baggage of wants
on the Skull's breast

He is free from attachments
to any outside influence
He lives only in the moment
the moment of fleshless existence
He has no decaying skin upon his brow
to hide the third eye
The Skull has the smile of all the sunrises
on his faceless face
His eyes cannot see
yet nothing passes him by

The Skull is free
The Skull is me
The Skull can be you
Just think it through
before you ask
for the glass mind
that shatters like glass

The Skull possesses
no judgment whatsoever
only the moment, wrapped in his bony hands
The Skull walks without fear
for what can hurt him?
Nothing, not even the mind of man
touches the Skull
There is no one for the Skull to impress
He just is

Unstruck Music from a Keyless Piano

Eat the world, my chelas
Eat the Mother's wrath
and become her love
in the moment
of consuming yourself in her form
For she is the image of chela
in that moment
of acceptance or rejection
When you consume her
her powers become pure love

Then the true dance begins
Unstruck music from a keyless piano
begins to be heard
and the Skull is born

The Skull is my Baba's Heart

The monkey was my companion
He taught me of the Skull
and the beauty of the Skull's fleshless spirit
the sockets that cannot see
yet can see more clearly than anyone
The lips that cannot speak
yet can lead one to the burning flame
of life's dhuni
The ears that cannot hear
yet miss nothing of life or death
The Skull is my Baba's heart

I feast my eyes on the nothingness of it all
So clear, so simple
To be skull-like without judgment or mind
is truly the place of the cremation grounds
that I wish my chelas to know best
The clear crackling of the fire
burning dead flesh
always sets my heart ablaze
with the balance
of flesh and ash and bones
Hanuman, Hanuman
my beloved Skull
I bow to the Servant of God

Silence

My Words Are Silent

Sometimes I long to sit in darshan
silent, in my own flowing juices

But my Baba says,
Your words, Ma, are silent
coming from a deep, silent well of truth
They quiet the living mind
and render the dead alive
Yesterday becomes today
and tomorrow does not exist
All is Maya
except for the light of death
around the Guru's being

The Silent Mind

I love Silence
Yes I, who talk so much
love infinite Silence
Silence without an end
Words can do a whole lot
but not as much as the silent heart
The mind always cheats you
out of your silent moments
The mind is always miserly
It is always a cheat
It is the ego-mind
that tries to limit my chelas in all things
especially things of a God-like nature
If you can be fearless even for a moment
you will taste a bliss
that will carry you to your Ma's feet

Who can do it for you?
No one, not even your Ma
And once you grasp the silent mind
you have that which cannot be lost
You are clinging to your minds
You must let the fingers of the ego
lose their touch on your heart

All that is great
comes from the death state of the ego
All that is splendor
comes from the silent mind
All that is beautiful
comes from the full heart

Silence

I sat in Silence
and worshipped you, my Baba

They all heard
my Silence
and became Silent, too

AGNI

The Lord of Fire, that which heats up the universe. He lies in the pit of the belly of human beings, the third chakra, and burns everything that comes before the holy one on the path to God. Agni takes in all things, good and bad, and uses them as fuel. When all is ash, the flame rises to the top of the head, shoots out of the Bhrahmarandra, and unites the human being with God. I bow to Agni in the dhunis we have on our ashram, in honor of this God of fire.

BABA

Baba is Neem Karoli Baba, my guru, not just in this life but in every life. He is the essence of purity, the essence of love, and, yes the essence of the Mother. Neem Karoli Baba's message to the world is to feed everyone. At Kashi Ashram we take his words to heart and give them life.

BURNING GHAT

The burning ghats in India are used to burn the bodies of the dead. My favorite one is the Manikarnika Ghat, with its steps going right down into the Ganga. The scent of burning flesh reminds one of the impermanence of all things, all things except God.

CHELA

The chela is the student of the guru. My guru says, "Chela is greater than guru, for he who can cast his eyes upon the guru's feet is greater than the guru."

DARSHAN

To see, to come and see, to receive, to take, to give, to give what you do not need in the receiving of what you do need. Darshan is to see the holy. Darshan is to become that which you see.

DHARMA

Dharma, a way of life, a way of life so exquisite it could
only run parallel with God's wishes. It is my dharma to
bring my chelas to God. It is in your dharma to come into
the great essence of love.

DHUNI

The sacred fire of Shiva which burns twenty-four hours a
day, reminding one that God's light is constantly burning
in our hearts.

DURGA

An aspect of the Divine Mother and consort of Lord Shiva.
The Goddess Durga is very special to us at Kashi Ashram,
where she presides in her own temple. She is so alive, so
dripping with life's nectar. I bow lowest to Mother Durga,
for through her, Kali was born. Through a light emanating
from her third eye, she gave birth to the Black Mother.

GANESH

The remover of all obstacles, he is called upon at the
beginning of all pujas. Ganesha Sharanam: I take refuge in
Ganesha, who will save me and all others.

GANGA, GANGAY, GANGES

The Ganga, the most sacred river in India. The Ganga is
my mother. The Ganga is my father. The Ganga is the
Earth's waters, Heaven's rain. The Ganga sits in the middle
of my ashram.

GOPI

The gopis are the women who loved and played with Lord
Krishna, on the banks of the sacred Yamuna River. A gopi
is a milkmaid, so beautiful, so clear of skin and eye, and

filled with such devotion. Being a gopi is an honor that should not be taken lightly.

GURU

There are not enough words to describe guru - he or she who is completely selfless, who casts no shadow upon his or her chelas, who walks upon this earth only to free the chela from the bonds of birth and death.

HANUMAN

Hanuman is the Monkey God - the magnificent, wonderful, furry Monkey God. He is Lord Shiva come to Earth to teach and preach of humility, having taken the form of a beast to do this great act. He is the Guru of Rama, and therefore he bows to Rama, for guru bows to chela.

JETTA

Shiva had jetta hair. Knots in the hair, hair that twirls on its own in honor of Lord Shiva. Lord Shiva's jetta locks touched the back of his waist.

KALI

Kali is the Dark Mother of the night. She is the wisdom of each and every god and goddess. She stalks the cremation ground devouring the flesh from the bone of ego. Kali is my mother; her power reigns inside of me. She is my love.

KRISHNA

My Lord Krishna, so blue of color, so gold of heart. The Lord plays upon his flute the melody that beckons all women to gather and find the passionate love one can have only for the Lord.

LAXMAN

Laxman to me, is my guru, Neem Karoli Baba, in his youth. But as recounted in the Ramayana, Laxman was

Rama's brother, who went with Rama on his journey into the forest when he was banned from Ayodhya

LONGOTI
Longoti is a piece of cloth wrapped around the groin of a Hindu man. Longoti is also the piece of cloth wrapped around my Lord Hanuman. It is usually red for Hanuman and white for a human.

MAYA
Maya is the Mother of Illusion. Illusion herself, or her daughter or son, lies inside a person's heart. You can pay attention to your heart and reach the core, or you can touch just the surface and reach illusion. Then the dance begins and nothing is real.

NAGAS
Nagas are the divine deities protecting all holy people as they sit inside their samadhi. A naga baba wears only his own flesh covered with ash. A naga was once a serpent who shed all his ego and became the divine naga.

PRANA
Prana is the very air we breathe in meditation, with great awareness, for then the air turns into the essence of God.

RISHIKESH
Rishikesh is a sacred city on the banks of the Ganga in India. In Rishikesh I learned the beauty and the soul of human beings. In Rishikesh I was with the first lepers who allowed me to be with them. I will remember it always.

SANNYAS
To take the vow of sannyas is to take one of a holy being. The vow of sannyas takes many forms. There are many

orders of sannyas. I took the vow of brahmacharya when I took the vow of sannyas at the feet of my guru. And I learned very simply it was not at all a vow of sacrifice. Everything came from my guru. Everything went to my guru. Everything still does. I am sannyasini.

SHAIVITE

Shaivite is the name of the sect of those who follow Shiva. Here at Kashi we are Shaivites. We follow Shiva in all his ways, or at least we do our best to comply to the wisdom of this great god. We are Shaivites who love Krishna and love all the gods. I wear the sacred ash every night of my life. I bow to my Lord Shiva as a Shaivite sannyasini.

SHIVA

Shiva, my Lord. Shiva, my guru. Shiva, my Baba. Shiva is he who destroys and rebuilds, he who eats the ego of his own children and gives birth through his own womb in the form of Kali.

(Shiva is part of the Hindu Trinity, along with Brahma and Vishnu. He is the master of creation and destruction; Shiva dreams the world as he sits in meditation.)

SKULL

The skull is an ancient tantric teaching. It represents what is bare and empty. I teach of the skull. The eyes that are no more yet can see all things. The nose that does not exist yet can smell all things. The mouth that is gone yet can say all things with a tongue that does not exist.

SWAMI

Swami is Swami Nityananda. The word "nityananda" means eternal bliss. The man, the god Nityananda, means many things, especially to me. He is my teacher. Like John

the Baptist, he prepared me for my guru. I sat at the feet of
Nityananda many lifetimes. He is the guru of the great
Swamiji Muktananda.

SUBEK

Subek is a word my guru said. All the same. It is all the
same. No difference. No difference. All things are the same.
Non-duality. Subek.

TARA

Mother Tara waits on the Manikarnika Ghat, waiting to
accept the ashes of her dead which she smears upon her
body so she will always remember those who will be reborn
to her feet.

VAYU

The wind, the god of the wind, the father of Hanuman.
Vayu very graciously and kindly touched Anjani and
impregnated her with a wisp of wind, forming his son in
her womb.

YAMA

The god of death, except when he is in Kashi, for there he
has no power whatsoever.

YAMUNA

The great river of Krishna. He danced upon her banks
making love to all the gopis.